Practical
Festive Food

p^3

This is a P³ Book
This edition published in 2003

P³
Queen Street House
4 Queen Street
Bath BA1 1HE, UK

Copyright © Parragon 2002

ISBN: 1-40542-313-7

Manufactured in China

NOTE

Cup measurements in this book are for American cups.
This book also uses imperial and metric measurements. Follow the same units
of measurement throughout; do not mix imperial and metric.
All spoon measurements are level: teaspoons are assumed to be 5 ml, and
tablespoons are assumed to be 15 ml. Unless otherwise stated,
milk is assumed to be whole milk, eggs and individual vegetables such as potatoes
are medium, and pepper is freshly ground black pepper.

The nutritional information provided for each recipe is per serving or per person.
Optional ingredients, variations, or serving suggestions have
not been included in the calculations. The times given for each recipe are an approximate
guide only because the preparation times may differ according to the techniques used by
different people and the cooking times may vary as a result of the type of oven used.

Recipes using raw or very lightly cooked eggs should be
avoided by infants, the elderly, pregnant women, convalescents,
and anyone suffering from an illness.

Contents

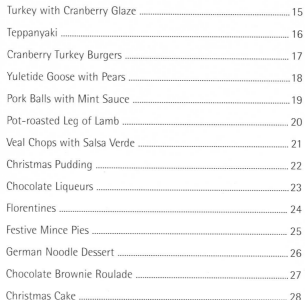

Pumpkin Soup

This American classic has now become popular worldwide. When pumpkin is out of season, use butternut squash in its place.

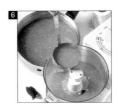

NUTRITIONAL INFORMATION	
Calories 112	Sugars 7g
Protein 4g	Fat 7g
Carbohydrate 8g	Saturates 2g

 10 mins   30 mins

SERVES 6

I N G R E D I E N T S

about 2 lb 4 oz/1 kg pumpkin

3 tbsp butter or margarine

1 onion, thinly sliced

1 garlic clove, crushed

3¾ cups vegetable bouillon

½ tsp ground ginger

1 tbsp lemon juice

3–4 thinly pared strips of orange zest (optional)

1–2 bay leaves or 1 bouquet garni

1¼ cups milk

salt and pepper

TO GARNISH

4–6 tbsp light or heavy cream, plain yogurt, or fromage frais

snipped fresh chives

1 Peel the pumpkin, remove the seeds, and then cut the flesh into 1-inch/2.5-cm cubes.

2 Melt the butter or margarine in a large, heavy-bottomed pan.

3 Add the sliced onion and crushed garlic and cook over low heat, until soft but not colored.

4 Add the pumpkin and toss with the onion for 2–3 minutes.

5 Add the bouillon and bring to a boil over medium heat. Season to taste with salt and pepper and add the ginger, lemon juice, strips of orange zest, if using, and the bay leaves or bouquet garni. Cover and simmer over low heat for about 20 minutes, until the pumpkin is tender.

6 Discard the orange zest, if using, and the bay leaves or bouquet garni. Cool the soup slightly, then press through a strainer or process in a food processor until smooth. Pour into a clean pan.

7 Pour in the milk and reheat gently. Adjust the seasoning. Garnish with a swirl of cream, plain yogurt, or fromage frais, top with snipped fresh chives, and serve.

Crab & Cabbage Soup

From the Vera Cruz region of Mexico, this delicious soup uses fresh crab meat to add a rich flavor to a mildly spicy vegetable and fish broth.

NUTRITIONAL INFORMATION

Calories	131	Sugars	10g
Protein	13g	Fat	4g
Carbohydrate	12g	Saturates	0g

🦀 25 mins   ⏱ 35 mins

SERVES 4

I N G R E D I E N T S

¼ cabbage

1 lb/450 g ripe tomatoes

4 cups fish bouillon, or 4 cups boiling water mixed with 1–2 fish bouillon cubes

1 onion, thinly sliced

1 small carrot, diced

4 garlic cloves, finely chopped

6 tbsp chopped fresh cilantro

1 tsp mild chili powder

1 whole cooked crab or 6–8 oz/175–225 g crab meat

1 tbsp torn fresh oregano leaves

salt and pepper

T O   S E R V E

1–2 limes, cut into wedges

salsa of your choice

1 Cut out and discard any thick stalks from the cabbage, then shred the leaves finely using a large knife.

2 To skin the tomatoes, place in a heatproof bowl, pour boiling water over to cover, and let stand for about 30 seconds. Drain and plunge into cold water. The skins will then slide off easily. Coarsely chop the skinned tomatoes.

3 Place the tomatoes and bouillon in a pan with the onion, carrot, cabbage, garlic, fresh cilantro, and chili powder. Bring to a boil, then lower the heat and simmer for about 20 minutes, until the vegetables are just tender.

4 If using whole crab, remove and reserve the crab meat. Twist off the legs and claws and crack with a heavy knife. Remove the flesh from the legs with a skewer; leave the cracked claws intact, if desired. Remove the body section from the main crab shell and remove the meat, discarding the stomach sac and feathery gills that lie along each side of the body.

5 Add the crab meat and oregano leaves to the pan and simmer for 10–15 minutes to combine the flavors. Season to taste with salt and pepper.

6 Ladle into deep soup bowls and serve immediately with 1–2 wedges of lime per serving. Hand around a bowl of your chosen salsa separately.

Baked Goat Cheese Salad

Scrumptious hot goat cheese and herb croûtes are served with a tossed leafy salad to make an excellent light snack, capturing Provençal flavors.

NUTRITIONAL INFORMATION

Calories	509	Sugars	. . . . .3g
Protein	. . . . .18g	Fat	. . . . .33g
Carbohydrate	. . .35g	Saturates	. . . . . .10g

 10 mins   🕙 10 mins

SERVES 4

I N G R E D I E N T S

9 oz/250 g mixed salad greens, such as arugula, mâche, and endive

12 slices French bread, plus extra to serve

extra-virgin olive oil, for brushing

12 thin slices of Provençal goat cheese, such as Picodon

fresh herbs, such as rosemary, thyme, or oregano, finely chopped

D R E S S I N G

6 tbsp extra-virgin olive oil

3 tbsp red wine vinegar

½ tsp sugar

½ tsp Dijon mustard

salt and pepper

1 To prepare the salad, rinse the leaves under cold water and pat dry with a dish towel. Wrap in paper towels and put in a plastic bag. Seal tightly and store in the refrigerator, until required.

2 To make the dressing, place all the ingredients in a screw-top jar and shake until well blended. Season with salt and pepper to taste and shake again. Set aside while preparing the croûtes.

3 Under a preheated broiler, toast the slices of French bread on both sides, until they are crisp. Brush a little olive oil on one side of each slice while they are still hot, so the oil is absorbed.

4 Place the croûtes on a cookie sheet and top each with a slice of cheese. Sprinkle the herbs over the cheese and drizzle with olive oil. Bake in a preheated oven, 350°F/180°C, for 5 minutes.

5 While the croûtes are in the oven, place the salad greens in a bowl. Shake the dressing again, pour it over the salad greens and toss together. Divide the salad between 4 plates.

6 Transfer the hot croûtes to the salad greens. Serve immediately with extra slices of French bread.

Tapenade

These robust olive and anchovy spreads can be as thick or as thin as you like. They make flavorful appetizers spread on toast.

NUTRITIONAL INFORMATION

Calories	227	Sugars	.........0g
Protein	.........5g	Fat	..........23g
Carbohydrate	....0g	Saturates	.......3g

   10–15 mins   5 mins

SERVES 6

I N G R E D I E N T S

thin slices of day-old baguette (optional)

olive oil (optional)

sprigs of fresh flatleaf parsley, to garnish

B L A C K   O L I V E   T A P E N A D E

2¼ cups black Niçoise olives in brine, rinsed and pitted

1 large garlic clove

2 tbsp walnut pieces

4 canned anchovy fillets, drained

about ½ cup extra-virgin olive oil

lemon juice, to taste

pepper

G R E E N   O L I V E   T A P E N A D E

2¼ cups green olives in brine, rinsed and pitted

4 canned anchovy fillets, rinsed

4 tbsp blanched almonds

1 tbsp capers in brine or vinegar, rinsed

about ½ cup extra-virgin olive oil

1½–3 tsp finely grated orange rind

pepper

1 To make the black olive tapenade, put the olives, garlic, walnut pieces, and anchovies in a food processor and process until blended.

2 With the motor running, slowly add the olive oil through the feeder tube, as if making mayonnaise. Add lemon juice and pepper to taste. Transfer to a bowl, cover with plastic wrap, and chill until required.

3 To make the green olive tapenade, put the olives, anchovies, almonds, and capers in a food processor and process until blended. With the motor running, slowly add the olive oil through the feeder tube, as if making mayonnaise. Add orange rind and pepper to taste. Transfer to a bowl, cover with plastic wrap, and chill until required.

4 To serve on croûtes, if desired, toast the slices of bread on both sides, until crisp. Brush 1 side of each slice with a little olive oil while they are still hot, so the oil is absorbed by the toast.

5 Spread the croûtes with the tapenade of your choice and garnish with parsley.

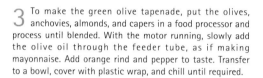

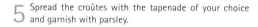

Mini Vegetable Puffs

These puffs look so impressive that they deserve to appear at the start of a formal meal. Yet they are surprisingly quick to make.

45 mins   20 mins

SERVES 4

I N G R E D I E N T S

1 lb/450 g puff pastry, defrosted if frozen

1 egg, beaten

F I L L I N G

8 oz/225 g sweet potato, cubed

3½ oz/100 g baby asparagus spears

2 tbsp butter

1 leek, sliced

2 small open-cap mushrooms, sliced

1 tsp lime juice

1 tsp chopped fresh thyme

pinch of dried mustard

salt and pepper

  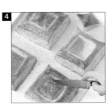

1 Cut the dough into 4 equal pieces. Roll each piece out on a lightly floured counter to form a 5-inch/13-cm square. Place on a dampened cookie sheet and score a smaller 3-inch/7.5-cm square inside each one.

2 Brush with beaten egg and cook in a preheated oven, 400°F/200°C, for 20 minutes, or until the puff pastry is risen and golden brown.

3 Meanwhile, make the filling. Cook the sweet potato in a pan of boiling water for 15 minutes, until tender. Drain well and set aside. Meanwhile, blanch the asparagus in another pan of boiling water for about 10 minutes, or until tender. Drain and reserve.

4 Remove the puff pastry squares from the oven, then carefully cut out the central square from each one with a sharp knife. Lift out and reserve.

5 Melt the butter in a pan, add the leek and mushrooms, and sauté for 2–3 minutes. Add the lime juice, thyme, and mustard, season well with salt and pepper, and stir in the sweet potatoes and asparagus. Spoon the mixture into the pastry shells, top with the reserved puff pastry squares, and serve immediately.

Mixed Nut Roast

Many consider this classic nut roast to be as traditional for vegetarians as turkey is for meat-eaters.

NUTRITIONAL INFORMATION

Calories	...628	Sugars	...34.1g
Protein	...13.8g	Fat	...43.7g
Carbohydrate	..47.9g	Saturates	...7.9g

🍲 30 mins   🕐 35 mins

SERVES 4

I N G R E D I E N T S

2 tbsp butter, plus extra for greasing

2 garlic cloves, chopped

1 large onion, chopped

½ cup hazelnuts, toasted and ground

½ cup walnuts, ground

⅓ cup cashews, ground

½ cup pine nuts, toasted and ground

scant 2 cups whole-wheat bread crumbs

1 egg, lightly beaten

2 tbsp chopped fresh thyme

1 cup vegetable bouillon

salt and pepper

CRANBERRY & RED WINE SAUCE

1¾ cups fresh cranberries

½ cup superfine sugar

1¼ cups red wine

1 cinnamon stick

sprigs of fresh thyme, to garnish

Brussels sprouts with buttered chestnuts, to serve

1 Preheat the oven to 350°F/180°C. Grease a loaf pan and line it with waxed paper. Melt the butter in a large pan over medium heat. Add the garlic and onion and cook, stirring, for 3 minutes, until softened. Remove from the heat and stir in the nuts, bread crumbs, egg, thyme, bouillon, and seasoning.

2 Spoon the mixture into the loaf pan and level the surface. Cook in the center of the preheated oven for 30 minutes or until cooked through and golden brown. The loaf is done when a skewer inserted into the center comes out clean. About halfway through the cooking time, make the sauce. Put all the ingredients into a pan and bring to a boil. Reduce the heat and simmer, stirring occasionally, for 15 minutes.

3 To serve, remove the sauce from the heat and discard the cinnamon stick. Remove the nut roast from the oven and turn out. Garnish with thyme; serve with the sauce and Brussels sprouts with buttered chestnuts.

Parmesan Potatoes

This is a very simple way to jazz up roast potatoes. The bacon and Parmesan cheese add a delicious flavor in this recipe.

NUTRITIONAL INFORMATION	
Calories 307	Sugars 2g
Protein 11g	Fat 14g
Carbohydrate . . .37g	Saturates 6g

15 mins   1 hr 5 mins

SERVES 4

INGREDIENTS

3 lb/1.3 kg potatoes

½ cup Parmesan cheese, grated

pinch of grated nutmeg

1 tbsp chopped fresh parsley

4 smoked bacon slices, cut into strips

vegetable oil, for roasting

salt

1 Cut the potatoes in half lengthwise and cook them in a pan of boiling salted water for 10 minutes. Drain them thoroughly.

2 Mix the grated Parmesan cheese, nutmeg, and parsley together in a shallow bowl.

3 Roll the potato pieces in the cheese mixture to coat them completely. Shake off any excess.

4 Pour a little oil into a roasting pan and heat it in a preheated oven, 400°F/200°C, for 10 minutes. Remove from the oven and place the potatoes in the pan. Return the pan to the oven and cook for 30 minutes, turning once.

5 Remove from the oven and scatter the bacon on top of the potatoes. Return to the oven for 15 minutes, or until the potatoes and bacon are cooked. Drain off any excess fat and serve.

VARIATION

If you prefer, use slices of salami or prosciutto instead of the bacon, adding it to the dish 5 minutes before the end of the cooking time.

Vegetable Hotchpotch

In this recipe, a variety of vegetables are arranged under a layer of potatoes, topped with cheese, and cooked until golden brown.

NUTRITIONAL INFORMATION

Calories	279	Sugars	........12g
Protein	........10g	Fat	...........11g
Carbohydrate	...34g	Saturates	.......4g

25 mins   1 hour

SERVES 4

I N G R E D I E N T S

2 large potatoes, thinly sliced

2 tbsp vegetable oil

1 red onion, halved and sliced

1 leek, sliced

2 garlic cloves, crushed

1 carrot, cut into chunks

3½ oz/100 g broccoli florets

3½ oz/100 g cauliflower florets

2 small turnips, cut into fourths

1 tbsp all-purpose flour

3 cups vegetable bouillon

⅔ cup hard cider

1 eating apple, cored and sliced

2 tbsp chopped fresh sage

pinch of cayenne pepper

½ cup grated colby cheese

salt and pepper

1 Cook the potato slices in a pan of boiling water for 10 minutes. Drain thoroughly and reserve.

2 Heat the oil in a flameproof casserole. Add the onion, leek, and garlic and sauté, stirring occasionally, for 2–3 minutes. Add the remaining vegetables and cook, stirring constantly, for another 3–4 minutes.

3 Stir in the flour and cook for 1 minute. Gradually pour in the bouillon and hard cider and bring to a boil. Add the apple, sage, and cayenne pepper and season well. Remove from the heat and transfer the vegetables to an ovenproof dish.

4 Arrange the potato slices on top of the vegetable mixture and cover evenly.

5 Sprinkle the cheese on top of the potato slices and cook in a preheated oven, 375°F/190°C, for 30–35 minutes, or until the potato is golden brown and beginning to go crisp around the edges. Serve immediately.

Winter Vegetable Pot Pie

Seasonal fresh vegetables are casseroled with lentils, then topped with a ring of fresh cheese biscuits to make this tasty pot pie.

NUTRITIONAL INFORMATION

Calories 734   Sugars 22g
Protein . . . . .27g   Fat 30g
Carbohydrate . . .96g   Saturates 16g

  20 mins   40 mins

SERVES 4

I N G R E D I E N T S

1 tbsp olive oil

1 garlic clove, crushed

8 small onions, halved

2 celery stalks, sliced

8 oz/225 g rutabaga, chopped

2 carrots, sliced

½ small cauliflower, broken into florets

3¼ cups sliced mushrooms

14 oz/400 g canned chopped tomatoes

¼ cup red lentils

2 tbsp cornstarch

3–4 tbsp water

1¼ cups vegetable bouillon

2 tsp Tabasco sauce

2 tsp chopped fresh oregano

sprigs of fresh oregano, to garnish

P O T   P I E   T O P P I N G

2 cups self-rising flour

4 tbsp butter

1 cup grated sharp colby cheese

2 tsp chopped fresh oregano

1 egg, lightly beaten

⅔ cup milk

salt

1 Heat the oil in a large skillet and cook the garlic and onions for 5 minutes. Add the celery, rutabaga, carrots, and cauliflower and cook for 2–3 minutes. Add the mushrooms, tomatoes, and lentils. Mix the cornstarch and water together and stir into the pan with the bouillon, Tabasco, and oregano. Transfer to a casserole and cover.

2 Bake in a preheated oven, 350°F/180°C, for 20 minutes.

3 To make the topping, sift the flour with a pinch of salt into a bowl. Rub in the butter, then stir in most of the cheese and the chopped oregano. Beat the egg with the milk and add enough to the dry ingredients to make a soft dough. Knead lightly, roll out to ½ inch/1 cm thick and cut into 2-inch/5-cm circles.

4 Remove the casserole from the oven and increase the temperature to 400°F/200°C. Arrange the biscuits around the edge of the casserole, brush with the remaining egg and milk, and sprinkle with the reserved cheese. Cook for another 10–12 minutes. Garnish and serve.

Traditional Roast Turkey

No Christmas would be complete without a turkey—here it is served with stuffing and complemented by a port and cranberry sauce.

NUTRITIONAL INFORMATION	
Calories 713	Sugars 30.8g
Protein 48g	Fat 36.7g
Carbohydrate . .50.8g	Saturates 15.3g

25 mins   3 hrs 20 mins

SERVES 4

I N G R E D I E N T S

6½–7¾ lb/3–3.5 kg oven-ready turkey

6 tbsp olive oil

1 garlic clove, finely chopped

scant ½ cup red wine

S T U F F I N G

3½ oz/100 g white mushrooms

1 onion, chopped

6 tbsp butter

1 garlic clove, chopped

scant 2 cups fresh bread crumbs

2 tbsp finely chopped fresh sage

1 tbsp lemon juice

salt and pepper

P O R T   &   C R A N B E R R Y   S A U C E

½ cup sugar

1 cup port

1¾ cups fresh cranberries

T O   S E R V E

roast garlic potatoes

spiced winter vegetables

1 Preheat the oven to 400°F/200°C. To make the stuffing, clean and chop the mushrooms, put them in a pan with the onion and butter and cook for 3 minutes. Remove from the heat and stir in the other ingredients. Rinse the turkey, pat dry with paper towels, fill the neck end with stuffing, and truss with string.

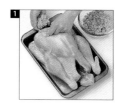

2 Pour the oil into a roasting dish and put the turkey in it. Rub the garlic over the bird and pour the wine over. Roast for 20 minutes. Baste, reduce the heat to 375°F/190°C, and roast for 40 minutes. Baste again and cover with foil. Roast for 2 hours, basting regularly. Check the bird is done by inserting a knife between the legs and body. If the juices run clear, it is done. Remove from the oven and let stand for 25 minutes. Meanwhile, put the sugar, port, and cranberries into a pan. Warm over medium heat until almost boiling. Reduce the heat, simmer for 15 minutes, stirring, then remove from the heat. Serve with the turkey and vegetables.

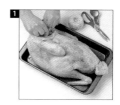

Turkey with Cheese Pockets

Wrapping strips of bacon around the turkey helps to keep the cheese filling enclosed in the pocket—and adds extra flavor.

NUTRITIONAL INFORMATION

Calories	518	Sugars	.........0g
Protein	........66g	Fat	..........28g
Carbohydrate	....0g	Saturates	.......9g

15 mins   20 mins

SERVES 4

I N G R E D I E N T S

4 turkey breasts, about 8 oz/225 g each

4 portions fullfat cheese (such as Bel Paese), ½ oz/15 g each

4 sage leaves or ½ tsp dried sage

8 strips rindless bacon

4 tbsp olive oil

2 tbsp lemon juice

salt and pepper

TO SERVE

garlic bread

salad greens

cherry tomatoes

1 Carefully cut a pocket into the side of each turkey breast. Open out each pocket a little and season inside with salt and pepper to taste.

2 Place a portion of cheese into each pocket, spreading it a little with a knife. Tuck a sage leaf into each pocket or sprinkle with a little dried sage.

3 Stretch out the bacon with the back of a knife. Wrap 2 pieces of bacon around each turkey portion, so that the pocket openings are completely covered.

4 Combine the oil and lemon juice in a small bowl.

5 Grill the turkey over medium hot coals for about 10 minutes on each side, basting frequently with the oil and lemon mixture.

6 Place the garlic bread at the side of the barbecue grill and toast lightly.

7 Transfer the turkey to warm serving plates. Serve with the toasted garlic bread, salad greens, and cherry tomatoes.

VARIATION

You can vary the cheese you use to stuff the turkey—try grated mozzarella or slices of Brie or Camembert. Also try placing 1 teaspoon of red currant jelly or cranberry sauce into each pocket instead of the sage.

Turkey with Cranberry Glaze

Traditional Thanksgiving ingredients are given a Chinese twist in this stir-fry, which contains cranberries, ginger, chestnuts, and soy sauce.

NUTRITIONAL INFORMATION

Calories	...167	Sugars	...11g
Protein	...8g	Fat	...7g
Carbohydrate	...20g	Saturates	...1g

5 mins   15 mins

SERVES 4

I N G R E D I E N T S

1 turkey breast

2 tbsp sunflower oil

2 tbsp preserved ginger

½ cup fresh or frozen cranberries

3½ oz/100 g canned chestnuts, drained

4 tbsp cranberry sauce

3 tbsp light soy sauce

salt and pepper

1 Remove any skin from the turkey breast. Using a sharp knife, thinly slice the flesh.

2 Heat the sunflower oil in a large, preheated wok or heavy-bottomed skillet.

3 Add the turkey to the wok and cook for 5 minutes, or until cooked through.

4 Using a sharp knife, finely chop the preserved ginger and add it to the pan.

5 Add the cranberries to the pan and cook for about 2–3 minutes, or until the cranberries have started to become soft.

6 Add the chestnuts, cranberry sauce, and soy sauce, season to taste with salt and pepper, and let the mixture bubble for 2–3 minutes.

7 Transfer the turkey stir-fry to warm serving bowls and serve immediately.

COOK'S TIP

It is very important that the wok is very hot before you cook. Test by holding your hand flat about 3 inches/7.5 cm above the bottom of the interior—you should be able to feel the heat radiating from it.

Teppanyaki

This simple, Japanese style of cooking is ideal for thinly sliced breast of chicken. You can use thin turkey scallops, if you prefer.

NUTRITIONAL INFORMATION	
Calories 206	Sugars 4g
Protein 30g	Fat 7g
Carbohydrate 6g	Saturates 2g

🔔 5 mins   🕐 10 mins

SERVES 4

I N G R E D I E N T S

4 boneless chicken breasts

1 red bell pepper

1 green bell pepper

4 scallions

8 baby corn cobs

3½ oz/100 g bean sprouts

1 tbsp sesame or sunflower oil

4 tbsp soy sauce

4 tbsp mirin (see Cook's Tip, below)

1 tbsp grated fresh gingerroot

1 Remove the skin from the chicken and slice the meat at a slight angle, to a thickness of about ¼ inch/5 mm.

2 Seed and thinly slice the red and green bell peppers and trim and slice the scallions and corn cobs.

3 Arrange the bell peppers, scallions, corn cobs, and bean sprouts on a plate with the sliced chicken.

4 Heat a large ridged grill pan, then lightly brush with sesame or sunflower oil. Add the vegetables and chicken slices, in small batches, leaving enough space between them so that they cook thoroughly.

5 Put the soy sauce, mirin, and ginger in a small serving bowl and stir together until combined. Serve as a dip with the chicken and vegetables.

COOK'S TIP

Mirin is a rich, sweet rice wine from Japan. You can buy it in Asian supermarkets, but if it is not available, add 1 tablespoon soft, light brown sugar to the sauce instead.

Cranberry Turkey Burgers

This recipe is bound to be popular with children and is very easy to prepare for their supper.

NUTRITIONAL INFORMATION

Calories	209	Sugars	........15g
Protein	........22g	Fat	..........5g
Carbohydrate	...21g	Saturates	......1g

45 mins   25 mins

SERVES 4

I N G R E D I E N T S

12 oz/350 g lean ground turkey

1 onion, finely chopped

1 tbsp chopped fresh sage

6 tbsp dry white bread crumbs

4 tbsp cranberry sauce

1 egg white, lightly beaten

2 tsp sunflower oil

salt and pepper

TO SERVE

4 toasted whole-wheat burger rolls

½ lettuce, shredded

4 tomatoes, sliced

4 tsp cranberry sauce

1 Combine the turkey, onion, sage, bread crumbs, and cranberry sauce in a bowl, and season to taste with salt and pepper. Mix in the egg white.

2 Using your hands, shape the mixture into four 4-inch/10-cm circles, about ¾ inch/2 cm thick. Chill for 30 minutes.

3 Line a broiler rack with baking parchment, making sure the ends are secured underneath the rack to ensure they do not catch fire. Place the burgers on top and brush lightly with oil. Put under a preheated moderate broiler and cook for 10 minutes. Turn the burgers over, brush again with oil. Broil them for another 12–15 minutes, until cooked through.

4 Fill each burger roll with lettuce, tomato, and a burger, and top with cranberry sauce.

COOK'S TIP

Look out for a variety of ready-ground meats at your butcher or supermarket. If unavailable, you can grind your own by choosing lean cuts and processing them in a blender or food processor.

Yuletide Goose with Pears

This Christmas favorite is as simple as it is delicious, with the goose surrounded by pears cooked in honey.

NUTRITIONAL INFORMATION		
Calories 651	Sugars 23.8g	
Protein 41.6g	Fat 43.9g	
Carbohydrate . .28.8g	Saturates 7.8g	

 20 mins   3–3¹/₂ hrs

SERVES 4

INGREDIENTS

7¾–10 lb/3.5–4.5 kg oven-ready goose

1 tsp salt

4 pears

1 tbsp lemon juice

4 tbsp butter

2 tbsp honey

lemon slices, to garnish

TO SERVE

roast garlic potatoes

spiced winter vegetables

Brussels sprouts with buttered chestnuts

honey-glazed red cabbage with golden raisins

1 Preheat the oven to 425°F/220°C. Rinse the goose and pat dry. Use a fork to prick the skin all over, then rub with salt. Place the bird upside down on a rack in a roasting pan. Roast for 30 minutes. Drain off the fat. Turn the bird over and roast for 15 minutes. Drain off the fat. Reduce the heat to 350°F/180°C and roast for 15 minutes per 1 lb/450 g.

Cover with foil 15 minutes before the end of the cooking time. Check the bird is done by inserting a knife between the legs and body. If the juices run clear, it is done. Remove from the oven.

2 Peel and halve the pears and brush with lemon juice. Melt the butter and honey in a pan over low heat, then add the pears. Cook, stirring, for 5–10 minutes, until tender. Remove from the heat, arrange the pears around the goose, and pour the sweet juices over the bird. Garnish with lemon slices and serve with garlic potatoes, winter vegetables, Brussels sprouts with buttered chestnuts, and red cabbage with golden raisins.

Pork Balls with Mint Sauce

Made with lean ground pork, the balls are first stir-fried, then braised in the wok with bouillon and pickled walnuts to give a tangy flavor.

NUTRITIONAL INFORMATION

Calories 318   Sugars 2g
Protein . . . . .30g   Fat 20g
Carbohydrate . . . .6g   Saturates 5g

5 mins   25 mins

SERVES 4

I N G R E D I E N T S

1 lb 2 oz/500 g lean ground pork

¾ cup fine fresh white bread crumbs

½ tsp ground allspice

1 garlic clove, crushed

2 tbsp chopped fresh mint

1 egg, beaten

2 tbsp sunflower oil

1 red bell pepper, seeded

generous 1 cup chicken bouillon

4 pickled walnuts, sliced

salt and pepper

sprigs of fresh mint, to garnish

rice or Chinese noodles, to serve

1 Combine the ground pork, bread crumbs, allspice, garlic, and half the chopped mint in a mixing bowl. Season to taste with salt and pepper, then bind together with the beaten egg.

2 Shape the meat mixture into 20 small balls with your hands, dampening your hands if it is easier for shaping.

3 Heat the sunflower oil in a wok or heavy skillet, swirling the oil around until really hot, then add the pork balls and stir-fry for about 4-5 minutes, or until browned all over.

4 Use a slotted spoon to remove the pork balls from the wok as they are cooked, then drain thoroughly on absorbent paper towels.

5 Pour off all but 1 tablespoon of fat and oil from the wok or skillet. Thinly slice the red bell pepper, then add to the pan and stir-fry for 2-3 minutes, or until the slices begin to soften but not color.

6 Add the chicken bouillon and bring to a boil. Season well with salt and pepper and return the pork balls to the wok, stirring well to coat in the sauce.

Simmer for 7-10 minutes, turning the pork balls from time to time.

7 Add the remaining chopped mint and the pickled walnuts to the wok and continue to simmer for 2-3 minutes, turning the pork balls regularly to coat them in the sauce.

8 Adjust the seasoning and serve the pork balls with rice or Chinese noodles or with a stir-fried vegetable dish, garnished with sprigs of fresh mint.

Pot Roasted Leg of Lamb

This dish from the Abruzzi region of Italy uses a slow cooking method. The meat absorbs the flavorings and becomes very tender.

NUTRITIONAL INFORMATION		
Calories 734	Sugars 6g	
Protein 71g	Fat 42g	
Carbohydrate 7g	Saturates 15g	

🍳 🍳 🍳

🥘 35 mins   🕐 3 hrs

SERVES 4

I N G R E D I E N T S

3 lb 8 oz/1.6 kg leg of lamb

3–4 sprigs of fresh rosemary

4 oz/115 g bacon strips

4 tbsp olive oil

2–3 garlic cloves, crushed

2 onions, sliced

2 carrots, sliced

2 celery stalks, sliced

1¼ cups dry white wine

1 tbsp tomato paste

1¼ cups bouillon

12 oz/350 g tomatoes, skinned, seeded, and cut into fourths

1 tbsp chopped fresh parsley

1 tbsp chopped fresh oregano or marjoram

salt and pepper

sprigs of fresh rosemary, to garnish

1 Wipe the joint of lamb all over, trimming off any excess fat, then season with salt and pepper, rubbing in well. Lay the sprigs of rosemary over the lamb, cover evenly with the bacon strips, and tie in place with string.

2 Heat the oil in a skillet and cook the lamb for about 10 minutes, turning several times. Remove from the skillet.

3 Transfer the oil from the skillet to a large, flameproof casserole and cook the garlic and onions for 3–4 minutes, until beginning to soften. Add the carrots and celery and cook for a few minutes longer.

4 Lay the lamb on top of the vegetables and press down to partly submerge. Pour the wine over the lamb, add the tomato paste, and simmer for about 3–4 minutes. Add the bouillon, tomatoes, and herbs, and season to taste with salt and pepper. Bring back to a boil for another 3–4 minutes.

5 Cover the casserole tightly and cook in a moderate oven, 350°F/180°C, for 2–2½ hours, until very tender.

6 Remove the lamb from the casserole and, if preferred, take off the bacon and herbs along with the string. Keep warm. Strain the juices, skimming off any excess fat, and serve in a pitcher. The vegetables may be arranged around the pot roast or in a serving dish. Garnish with sprigs of fresh rosemary.

Veal Chops with Salsa Verde

This vibrant, green Italian sauce adds a touch of Mediterranean flavor to any simply cooked meat or seafood.

NUTRITIONAL INFORMATION

Calories 481	Sugars 1g
Protein 41g	Fat 34g
Carbohydrate 2g	Saturates 5g

🍳 10 mins   🕐 5 mins

SERVES 4

I N G R E D I E N T S

4 veal chops, such as loin chops, about 8 oz/225 g each and ¾ inch/2 cm thick

garlic-flavored olive oil, for brushing

salt and pepper

fresh oregano or basil leaves, to garnish

S A L S A   V E R D E

2 cups fresh flatleaf parsley leaves

3 canned anchovy fillets in oil, drained

1½ tsp capers in brine, rinsed and drained

1 shallot, finely chopped

1 garlic clove, halved, green core removed, and chopped

1 tbsp lemon juice

6 large, fresh basil leaves or ¾ tsp freeze-dried basil

2 sprigs of fresh oregano or ½ tsp dried oregano

½ cup extra-virgin olive oil

1. To make the salsa verde, put the parsley, anchovies, capers, shallot, garlic, lemon juice, basil, and oregano in a blender or food processor and process until they are thoroughly chopped and blended.

2. With the motor running, add the oil through the top or feeder tube and process until thickened. Season with pepper to taste. Scrape into a bowl, cover with plastic wrap, and chill in the refrigerator.

3. Lightly brush the veal chops with olive oil and season to taste with salt and pepper. Place under a preheated broiler and cook for about 3 minutes. Turn over, brush with more oil, and broil for another 2 minutes, until cooked when tested with the tip of a knife.

4. Transfer the chops to warmed individual plates and spoon a little of the chilled salsa verde beside them. Garnish the chops with fresh oregano or basil and serve with the remaining salsa verde handed separately.

COOK'S TIP
The salsa verde will keep for up to 2 days in a covered container in the refrigerator. It is also marvelous served with broiled red snapper.

Christmas Pudding

This timeless, classic pudding is an essential part of the Christmas table. Make it well in advance, because it needs to chill for at least two weeks.

NUTRITIONAL INFORMATION			
Calories 1273	Sugars 150.4g
Protein 20.6g	Fat 51g
Carbohydrate ..197g	Saturates 25.3g

🥮 2¼ hrs   🕐 8 hrs + 2–8 weeks to chill

SERVES 4

I N G R E D I E N T S

1⅓ cups currants

scant 1⅓ cups raisins

scant 1¼ cups golden raisins

⅔ cup sweet sherry

¾ cup butter, plus extra for greasing

generous ¾ cup brown sugar

4 eggs, beaten

generous 1 cup self-rising flour

scant 2 cups fresh white or
    whole-wheat bread crumbs

⅓ cup blanched almonds, chopped

juice of 1 orange

grated zest of ½ orange

grated zest of ½ lemon

½ tsp ground allspice

holly leaves, to decorate

1 Put the currants, raisins, and golden raisins into a glass bowl and pour over the sherry. Let soak for at least 2 hours.

2 Mix the butter and sugar in a bowl. Beat in the eggs, then fold in the flour. Stir in the soaked fruit and sherry with the bread crumbs, almonds, orange juice and zest, lemon zest, and allspice. Grease an ovenproof bowl and press the mixture into it, leaving a gap of 1 inch/2.5 cm at the top. Cut a circle of waxed paper 1½ inches/3 cm larger than the top of the bowl, grease with butter, and place over the pudding. Secure with string, then top with 2 layers of foil. Place the pudding in a pan filled with boiling water which reaches two-thirds of the way up the bowl. Reduce the heat and simmer for 6 hours, topping up the water when necessary.

3 Remove from the heat and let cool. Renew the waxed paper and foil and refrigerate for 2–8 weeks. To reheat, steam for 2 hours as before. Decorate with holly and serve.

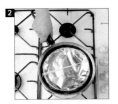

Chocolate Liqueurs

These tasty chocolate cups are filled with a delicious liqueur-flavored filling. Use your favorite liqueur to flavor the cream.

🍰 1 hr   🕐 5 mins

MAKES 40

INGREDIENTS

3½ oz/100 g dark chocolate

about 5 candied cherries, halved

about 10 hazelnuts or macadamia nuts

⅔ cup heavy cream

2 tbsp confectioners' sugar

4 tbsp liqueur

TO FINISH

1¾ oz/50 g dark chocolate, melted

a little white chocolate, melted, or white chocolate curls, or extra nuts and cherries

1 Line a cookie sheet with a sheet of baking parchment. Break the dark chocolate into pieces, place in a heatproof bowl, and set over a pan of hot water. Stir until melted. Spoon the chocolate into 20 paper candy cases, spreading up the sides with a small spoon or brush. Place upside down on the cookie sheet and let set.

2 Carefully peel away the paper cases. Place a cherry or nut in each cup.

3 To make the filling, place the heavy cream in a mixing bowl and sift the confectioners' sugar on top. Whisk the cream until it is just holding its shape, then whisk in the liqueur.

4 Place the cream in a pastry bag fitted with a ½-inch/1-cm plain tip and pipe a little into each chocolate case. Let chill for 20 minutes.

5 To finish, spoon the melted dark chocolate over the cream to cover it.

Pipe the melted white chocolate on top, swirling it into the dark chocolate with a toothpick. Let the candies harden. Alternatively, cover the cream with the melted dark chocolate and decorate with white chocolate curls before setting. Or place a small piece of nut or candied cherry on top of the cream, then cover with melted dark chocolate.

COOK'S TIP
Candy cases can vary in size. Use the smallest you can find for this recipe.

Florentines

These luxury cookies will be popular at any time of the year, but they make a particularly marvelous treat at Thanksgiving.

NUTRITIONAL INFORMATION			
Calories	209	Sugars	........20g
Protein	.........2g	Fat	..........12g
Carbohydrate	...26g	Saturates	......6g

 50 mins   10 mins

MAKES 10

I N G R E D I E N T S

4 tbsp butter

¼ cup superfine sugar

scant ¼ cup all-purpose flour, sifted

⅓ cup almonds, chopped

⅓ cup chopped candied mixed peel

¼ cup raisins, chopped

2 tbsp chopped candied cherries

zest of ½ lemon, finely grated

4½ oz/125 g dark chocolate, melted

1 Line 2 large cookie sheets with baking parchment.

2 Heat the butter and superfine sugar in a small pan, until the butter has just melted and the sugar has dissolved. Remove the pan from the heat.

3 Stir in the flour and mix well. Stir in the chopped almonds, mixed peel, raisins, cherries, and lemon zest. Place teaspoonfuls of the mixture well apart on the cookie sheets.

4 Bake in a preheated oven, 350°F/ 180°C, for 10 minutes, or until they are lightly golden.

5 As soon as the florentines are removed from the oven, use a cookie cutter to press the edges into neat shapes while still on the cookie sheets. Let cool on the cookie sheets, until firm, then transfer to a wire rack to cool completely.

6 Spread the melted chocolate over the smooth side of each florentine. As the chocolate begins to set, mark wavy lines in it with a fork. Let the florentines set, chocolate side up.

VARIATION
Replace the dark chocolate with white chocolate or, for a dramatic effect, cover half of the florentines in dark chocolate and half in white.

Festive Mince Pies

Serve these seasonal pastries with spiced mulled wine or eggnog. The filling is very hot when the pies come out of the oven, so let them cool.

NUTRITIONAL INFORMATION

Calories 201	Sugars 18g
Protein 2g	Fat 8.6g
Carbohydrate . .30.7g	Saturates 4.5g

20 mins   15 mins

MAKES 12

INGREDIENTS

scant 1½ cups all-purpose flour, plus extra for dusting

scant ½ cup butter

¼ cup confectioners' sugar, plus extra for dusting

1 egg yolk

2–3 tbsp milk

10½ oz/300 g mincemeat

1 egg, beaten, for sealing and glazing

sprigs of holly, to decorate

 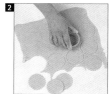 

1 Preheat the oven to 350°F/180°C. Sift the flour into a mixing bowl. Using your fingertips, rub in the butter until the mixture resembles bread crumbs. Mix in the sugar and egg yolk. Stir in enough milk to make a soft dough, turn out onto a lightly floured counter, and knead lightly until smooth.

2 Shape the dough into a ball and roll out to a thickness of ½ inch/ 1 cm. Use fluted cutters to cut out 12 circles of 2¾ inches/7 cm diameter and 12 circles of 2 inches/5 cm diameter. Dust 12 tartlet pans with flour and line with the larger dough circles. Prick the bottoms with a fork, then half-fill each pie with mincemeat. Brush beaten egg around the rims, then press the smaller dough circles on top to seal. Make a small hole in the top of each one. Decorate the pies with Christmas trees made from dough trimmings. Brush all over with beaten egg, then bake for 15 minutes. Remove from the oven and cool on a wire rack. Dust with confectioners' sugar and serve.

German Noodle Dessert

This rich and satisfying dessert is based on a traditional Jewish recipe, and makes a delicious finale to any meal.

NUTRITIONAL INFORMATION

Calories	721	Sugars	........27g
Protein	........21g	Fat	..........45g
Carbohydrate	...63g	Saturates	.....24g

 15 mins   🕐 50 mins

SERVES 4

INGREDIENTS

4 tbsp butter, plus extra for greasing

6 oz/175 g ribbon egg noodles

½ cup cream cheese

1 cup cottage cheese

scant ½ cup superfine sugar

2 eggs, lightly beaten

½ cup sour cream

1 tsp vanilla extract

pinch of ground cinnamon

1 tsp grated lemon zest

¼ cup slivered almonds

1 oz/25 g dry white bread crumbs

confectioners' sugar, for dusting

1 Grease an ovenproof dish with a little butter.

2 Bring a large pan of water to a boil. Add the noodles and cook until almost tender. Drain and set aside.

3 Beat together the cream cheese, cottage cheese, and superfine sugar in a mixing bowl. Beat in the eggs, a little at a time. Stir in the sour cream, vanilla extract, cinnamon, and lemon zest, and fold in the noodles. Transfer the mixture to the prepared dish and then smooth the surface.

4 Melt the remaining butter in a skillet. Add the almonds and cook, stirring constantly, for about 1–1½ minutes, until lightly colored. Remove the skillet from the heat and stir the bread crumbs into the almonds.

5 Sprinkle the almond and bread crumb mixture over the top and bake in a preheated oven at 350°F/180°C for about 35–40 minutes, until just set. Dust with a little confectioners' sugar and then serve immediately.

VARIATION

Although not authentic, you could add 3 tablespoons raisins with the lemon zest in step 3, if you wish.

Chocolate Brownie Roulade

This delicious dessert is inspired by chocolate brownies. The addition of nuts and raisins gives it extra texture.

NUTRITIONAL INFORMATION

Calories 436	Sugars 38g	
Protein 7g	Fat 30g	
Carbohydrate . . .38g	Saturates 16g	

45 mins   25 mins

SERVES 8

INGREDIENTS

2 tsp melted butter, for greasing

5½ oz/150 g semisweet chocolate, broken into pieces

3 tbsp water

generous ¾ cup superfine sugar

5 eggs, separated

scant ¼ cup raisins, chopped

scant ¼ cup pecans, chopped

pinch of salt

confectioners' sugar, for dusting

1¼ cups heavy cream, lightly whipped

1 Grease a 12 x 8-inch/30 x 20-cm jelly roll pan with butter, line with baking parchment, and grease the parchment.

2 Place the chocolate, with the water, in a small pan over low heat, stirring until the chocolate has just melted. Let cool a little.

3 In a bowl, whisk the sugar and egg yolks for 2–3 minutes with an electric whisk, until thick and pale. Fold in the cooled chocolate, raisins, and pecans.

4 In a separate bowl, whisk the egg whites with the salt. Fold one fourth of the egg whites into the chocolate mixture, then fold in the rest of the whites, working lightly and quickly.

5 Transfer the cake batter to the prepared pan and bake in a preheated oven, 350°F/180°C, for 25 minutes, until risen and just firm to the touch. Let cool before covering with a sheet of nonstick baking parchment and a damp, clean dish towel. Let the cake stand until completely cold before filling and rolling.

6 Turn onto another piece of baking parchment dusted with confectioners' sugar. Remove the lining parchment.

7 Spread the whipped cream over the roulade. Starting from a short end, roll the sponge away from you, using the paper as a guide. Trim the ends of the roulade to a neat finish and transfer to a serving plate. Let the roulade chill in the refrigerator until ready to serve. Dust with a little more confectioners' sugar.

Christmas Cake

Christmas would not be the same without a traditional fruitcake.
This one is decorated with a delicious lemony white frosting.

NUTRITIONAL INFORMATION

Calories	236	Sugars	......34.7g
Protein	........2.6g	Fat	..........8.2g
Carbohydrate	..40.6g	Saturates	.....4.3g

45 mins
plus 8 hrs
to soak

3 hrs

MAKES ONE 8-INCH/20-CM CAKE

I N G R E D I E N T S

scant 1 cup raisins

generous ⅔ cup pitted dates, chopped

generous ⅔ cup golden raisins

½ cup candied cherries, rinsed

⅔ cup brandy

1 cup butter, plus extra for greasing

1 cup superfine sugar

4 eggs

grated zest of 1 orange and 1 lemon

1 tbsp molasses

generous 1½ cups all-purpose flour

½ tsp salt

½ tsp baking powder

1 tsp allspice

scant ¼ cup toasted almonds, chopped

scant ¼ cup toasted hazelnuts, chopped

F R O S T I N G

1 egg white

juice of 1 lemon

1 tsp vanilla extract

4½ cups confectioners' sugar

holly leaves, to decorate

1 Make this cake at least 3 weeks in advance. Put all the fruit in a bowl, pour over the brandy, and soak overnight.

2 Preheat the oven to 225°F/110°C. Grease an 8-inch/20-cm cake pan and line it with waxed paper. In a bowl, cream together the butter and sugar until fluffy. Gradually beat in the eggs. Stir in the citrus zest and molasses. In a separate bowl, sift together the flour, salt, baking powder, and allspice, then fold into the egg mixture. Fold in the fruit, brandy, and nuts, then spoon into the cake pan. Bake for at least 3 hours. If it browns too quickly, cover with foil. The cake is cooked when a skewer inserted into the center comes out clean. Remove from the oven and cool on a wire rack. Store in an airtight container until required.

3 To make the frosting, put the egg white, lemon juice, vanilla extract, and sugar into a bowl and mix until smooth. Spread over the cake, using a fork to give texture. Decorate with holly leaves.